Table of Contents

About Antarctica

Antarctica lies at the southern end of the world. It is the fifth biggest **continent**. Its land is covered in thick ice and surrounded by the Southern Ocean. Around Antarctica, parts of the ocean freeze over in winter.

PACIFIC OCEAN

continent—one of Earth's seven large land masses

CONTINENTS OF THE WORLD

ARCTIC OCEAN

NORTH AMERICA

EUROPE

ASIA

ATLANTIC OCEAN

AFRICA

EQUATOR

INDIAN OCEAN

SOUTH AMERICA

AUSTRALIA

SOUTHERN OCEAN

ANTARCTICA

Famous Places

Antarctica often is called the South Pole. The South Pole is an actual spot on Antarctica. A sign is placed there as a marker. Even though it is very cold, a U.S. research station is nearby.

Mount Erebus is a mountain on Ross Island in the Ross Sea. It is an active **volcano**. That means it often erupts, shooting out rocks and steam.

Fact: Mount Erebus is 12,447 feet (3,794 meters) high.

volcano–an opening in the earth's surface that sometimes sends out hot lava, steam, and ash

A sign marks the South Pole.

Geographic South Pole

Roald Amundsen
December 14 1911
"So we arrived and were able to plant our flag at the geographical South Pole."

Robert F. Scott
January 17, 1912
"The Pole. Yes, but under very different circumstances from those expected."

elevation 9,301 feet

Mount Erebus

Geography

Antarctica is mostly covered by a sheet of ice. Glaciers flow very slowly from the ice sheet into the ocean. A glacier is a large piece of slow-moving ice.

Huge shelves of ice hang over the ocean around Antarctica. Sometimes chunks of ice break off these shelves and the glaciers. They float in the ocean as icebergs.

Fact: In some places, Antarctica's ice is 3 miles (5 kilometers) thick.

glacier

Antarctica also has mountains. The Transantarctic Mountains run across the continent. The tops of the mountains stick out above Antarctica's sheet of ice. Vinson Massif is in the Ellsworth Mountains. It is the highest mountain on the continent.

Ellsworth Mountains

Many large lakes are under the ice. Lake Vostok is under 2.5-mile (4-km) thick ice. The water in the lake is still liquid.

Fact: Vinson Massif is 16,067 feet (4,897 meters) high.

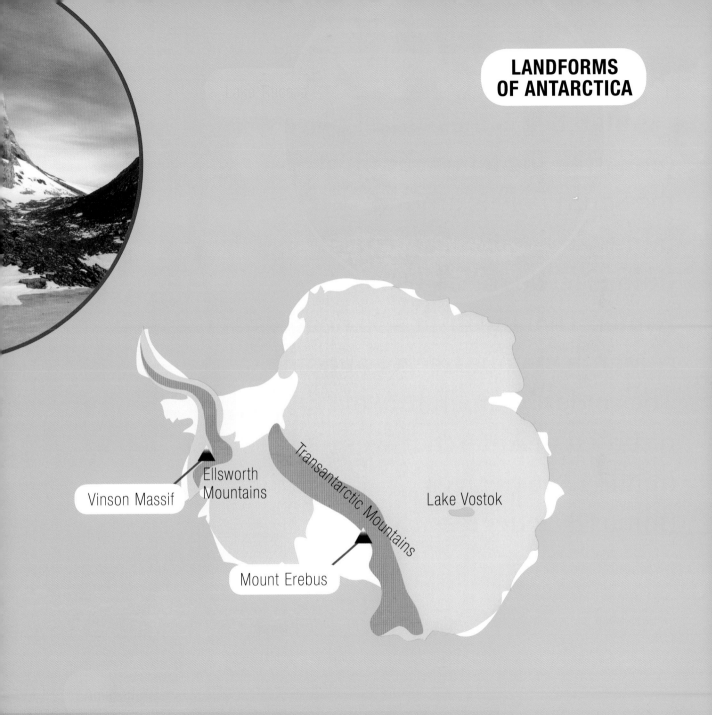

Vinson Massif

Ellsworth Mountains

Transantarctic Mountains

Mount Erebus

Lake Vostok

Weather

Antarctica is the coldest place on Earth. The temperature at the South Pole is around minus 76 degrees Fahrenheit (minus 60 degrees Celsius) in winter. That means it's 56 degrees colder than your freezer at home. The coldest temperature ever recorded in Antarctica was minus 128.6 degrees F (minus 89.2 degrees C).

Wind whips snow across Antarctica's frozen land.

Antarctica is the windiest place in the world. Strong storms called blizzards happen often. Blizzards occur when the wind blows snow around. It is hard to move or see during a blizzard.

Fact: Parts of the Southern Ocean freeze in winter. This causes Antarctica to grow almost twice in size.

Scientists use snow vehicles called Hagglunds to travel over Antarctica.

Animals

Penguins, whales, and seals live in and around Antarctica. These animals have a thick layer of fat under their skin. The fat keeps them warm. Weddell seals swim under the ocean ice. They chew holes in the ice. Then they can reach the surface to breathe.

penguins

Weddell seals

People

Antarctica is the only continent that does not have its own countries. People from many other countries work together to study and look after Antarctica. Scientists live for a few months at a time at research stations. They study the continent's ice, rocks, weather, animals, and plants.

Fact: The first person to reach the South Pole was explorer Roald Amundsen in 1911. He used dogs to pull sleds across the continent.

Scientists study water on Antarctica.

Argentina's research station in Antarctica

Natural Resources

Thousands of **tourists** visit Antarctica every year. They come to see the animals and frozen land. Besides tourism, Antarctica has **resources** such as coal, oil, and minerals. These lie deep under the ice. People cannot mine or drill for the resources because doing so could damage this amazing continent.

tourist—a person who travels and visits places for fun or adventure

resource—something useful or valuable to people

Glossary

continent (KAHN-tuh-nuhnt)—one of Earth's seven large land masses

resource (REE-sorss)—something useful or valuable to people

tourist (TOOR-ist)—a person who travels and visits places for fun or adventure

volcano (vol-KAY-noh)—an opening in the earth's surface that sometimes sends out hot lava, steam, and ash

Read More

Bluthenthal, Todd. *The South Pole*. Where on Earth? New York: Gareth Stevens Publishing, 2018.

Roumanis, Alexis. *Antarctica*. Exploring the Continents. New York: AV2 by Weigl, 2016.

Internet Sites

Use FactHound to find Internet sites related to this book.

Visit *www.facthound.com*

Just type in 9781543527957 and go.

 Check out projects, games and lots more at
www.capstonekids.com

Critical Thinking Questions

1. Antarctica is the coldest place on Earth. What features do animals have to keep warm there?

2. Antarctica does not have any countries. Who takes care of Antarctica?

3. Describe why tourists might visit Antarctica.

Index

Download the Capstone 4D app!

- Ask an adult to download the Capstone 4D app.

- Scan the cover and stars inside the book for additional content.

When you scan a spread, you'll find
fun extra stuff to go with this book!
You can also find these things
on the web at www.capstone4D.com
using the password: antarctica.27957

First Facts are published by Pebble,
1710 Roe Crest Drive, North Mankato, Minnesota 56003
www.mycapstone.com

Library of Congress Cataloging-in-Publication Data
Library of Congress Cataloging-in-Publication Data is on file with the Library of the Congress.
ISBN 978-1-5435-2795-7 (library binding)
ISBN 978-1-5435-2801-5 (paperback)
ISBN 978-1-5435-2807-7 (ebook pdf)

Editorial Credits
Cynthia Della-Rovere and Clare Webber, designers; Svetlana Zhurkin, media researcher;
Kathy McColley, production specialist

Photo Credits
Capstone Global Library Ltd, 5, 11; Dreamstime: Maxily, 19 (back); Getty Images: Thomas Pickardgraher, 15; Shutterstock: Alexey Seafarer, cover (bottom left), Armin Rose, 21, ArTDi101 (pattern), cover (left) and throughout, Christopher Wood, 9, evenfh, cover (middle), 17 (back), Harvepino, cover (bottom right), back cover, 1, 3, Jeff Warneck, 7 (inset), K Ireland, cover (top), polarman, 7 (back), 19 (inset), robert mcgillivray, 13, Roger Clark ARPS, 10, Sergey 402, 17 (inset)

Printed and bound in the USA.   PA017

First
Facts®

Investigating
CONTINENTS

ANTARCTICA

A 4D Book

by Christine Juarez

PEBBLE
a capstone imprint